The Ge

Guide

**30 Things Every 21st Century Gentleman
Should Know and Do**

Kareem J. Hayes

No portion of this book may be reproduced in any form,

except for brief quotations in reviews, without written

permission from the author.

This book is dedicated to my father and all of the great men in my life who were examples of what it meant to be a gentleman. Also, I would like to dedicate this book to my dear wife Brandi who was an inspiration for putting this literature together and my two beautiful children Chloe and Kareem Jr.

Forward

The purpose of this book is to provide you with the essential ingredients for being a 21st century gentleman. It is my hope that you will use this book as a guide to setting yourself apart from the pack. Being a gentleman isn't just about wearing the occasional suit, but having the attitude to go with the clothing.

Chivalry isn't widely taught in most schools or homes anymore and this has to change. The most important possession that we all have is our name and how people remember us. If you are reading this book then you care about your name and what you stand for as an individual.

Lastly, I hope this book will spur conversation between your fellow man and that you will develop a hunger to own the wisdom provided in this book. Cheers.

Sincerely,

Kareem J. Hayes

Letter To The Reader

There was a time in our culture when being a gentleman was the norm instead of the exception. Fathers taught their sons to be providers, protectors, and priests of their homes and communities. Men carried themselves with dignity and boys looked on in awe with the hopes of one day being able to pick up the torch to propagate what was demonstrated to them.

But there has been a breakdown in society. Instead of having strong positive role models set before our young men, the extreme opposite has become the object of their gaze. Disrespect of women is glorified and clear strong articulation is substituted for demeaning low level language. Well-dressed groomed men have been deemed as old fashioned and sagging pants with colorful boxers is displayed as what's "in". Where do we go from here?

Kareem has provided some foundational and necessary tips for young men to follow. He's taken the wisdom of our fathers and placed it into the hands of a generation of boys that will benefit from it greatly. This can be the beginning of the turning of our young boys! Manners, respect, and chivalry can once again be the norm instead of the exception. The gentleman will ALWAYS be in style! *30 Things Every 21st Gentleman Should Know and Do* is sure to put every young man who reads it on the right path to a bright future.

Melvin Cross Jr. M.Div
Senior Pastor, Glory House International

30 Things Every 21st Century Gentleman Should Know and Do

1.

Give Thanks

Give thanks to God when you wake up in the morning because no day is promised to us. There are people everyday who are not waking up on this side of paradise. We need to show appreciation for having another day to live in purpose and fulfilling destiny.

What are some ways you can give
thanks or show appreciation?

_____

_____

_____

_____

_____

_____

_____

_____

_____

_____

_____

_____

_____

_____

_____

_____

_____

_____

2.

Say Good Morning

Say good morning to people even if

you don't feel like it. As a

gentleman, take the initiative to set

the tone in the morning for having a

good and productive day. Saying

good morning is a great way to start

the day and show people that you

are friendly

Why do you think saying good morning
is important?

_____

_____

_____

_____

_____

_____

_____

_____

_____

_____

_____

_____

_____

_____

_____

_____

_____

3.

Focus and Strategize

Look at your phone after you get

dressed for the day and focus on

your day ahead. Whatever is on

your phone will be there after you

get dressed. It's important to take

some time to think and strategize

What would you do if you didn't have your phone for 24 hours? Would you be able to function without it?

_____

_____

_____

_____

_____

_____

_____

_____

_____

_____

_____

_____

_____

_____

_____

_____

4.

Firm Handshake

When you shake a man's hand, look him in the eye so he can know you mean business. There's nothing worse than someone giving you a weak handshake and not looking you in your eyes.

Has anyone ever given you a weak handshake? What does looking someone in their eyes signify?

_____

_____

_____

_____

_____

_____

_____

_____

_____

_____

_____

_____

_____

_____

_____

_____

_____

5.

Respect Your Elders

Speak to adults when you see them and acknowledge their presence. After all, they are your elders and deserve your respect. One day you may need them for their wisdom and experience.

How would you feel if someone disrespected your grandparents? What would be your reaction? Are you guilty of being disrespectful to elderly people?

_____

_____

_____

_____

_____

_____

_____

_____

_____

_____

_____

_____

_____

_____

_____

_____

6.

Show Some Courtesy

Give up your seat to a lady or an elderly person if they are standing and have nowhere to sit. It's the right thing to do. Remember, what goes around, comes around and one day you will get old and need a chair to rest your legs.

Can you recall a time when you gave up your seat for an elderly person? How do you think the individual felt? How did you feel about it?

_____

_____

_____

_____

_____

_____

_____

_____

_____

_____

_____

_____

_____

_____

_____

_____

7.

Family Business

Talk positively about your family because you are a reflection of them. Family business is family business and everyone doesn't need to know all of it. Learn to practice discretion when having casual conversations with people.

Is family important to you? Why?

_____

_____

_____

_____

_____

_____

_____

_____

_____

_____

_____

_____

_____

_____

_____

_____

_____

8.

Blessed Are Those Who Respect Authority

Respect those who have authority

over you because they are in that

position for a reason. Gentlemen are

able to be led by those in authority

and are teachable. Being teachable

can afford you opportunities for

growth and promotion.

Do you have an issue with respecting authority? Can you name a time when you had a conflict with someone who had authority over you? How did you handle it?

_____

_____

_____

_____

_____

_____

_____

_____

_____

_____

_____

_____

_____

_____

_____

_____

9.

Think Before You Speak

Think before you speak because it shows that you have some common sense and self-control. Those who speak without thinking are looked at by their peers as foolish and incompetent. This also includes the use of vulgar language because it's just plain rude and shows a lack of respect.

Have you ever said something before thinking about it and it came back to haunt you? Give an example. What did you learn from the experience?

_____

_____

_____

_____

_____

_____

_____

_____

_____

_____

_____

_____

_____

_____

_____

_____

10.

Decline With Grace

Decline an offer with grace and
poise. You do not have to make a
scene about it by drawing
unnecessary attention. Gentlemen
are not rude and do their best to
preserve another person's
reputation.

Think about a time when you had to decline a gift? How did you handle it?

_____

_____

_____

_____

_____

_____

_____

_____

_____

_____

_____

_____

_____

_____

_____

_____

_____

_____

_____

11.

An Invitation to Dinner

If you are asked to eat dinner with a family, take them on their offer because they deem you as worthy to break bread with them. Having dinner is an opportunity to converse and build relationship.

Have you ever been invited over to a friend's house for dinner? What was your experience?

_____

_____

_____

_____

_____

_____

_____

_____

_____

_____

_____

_____

_____

_____

_____

_____

12.

Open The Door

Open the door for an elderly person and a lady. It is a sign of respect and chivalry. Would you want someone to hold the door for your mother? Part of being chivalrous is thinking about others before yourself.

What does chivalry mean? Do you consider yourself to be chivalrous?

_____

_____

_____

_____

_____

_____

_____

_____

_____

_____

_____

_____

_____

_____

_____

_____

_____

_____

_____

_____

13.

Répondez S'il Vous Plaît

When you are invited to an event, make sure you reserve your attendance and offer to help. There's nothing worse than showing up to an event unannounced and unaccounted for. Please be kind and respond to your RSVP.

Have you ever had to RSVP for an event? What were the instructions? How did you follow through?

_____

_____

_____

_____

_____

_____

_____

_____

_____

_____

_____

_____

_____

_____

_____

_____

14.

Don't Eat Like a Caveman

When eating, make sure that you eat with your mouth closed. No one else should be able to see or hear what you are eating. It's good to have proper eating habits and etiquette. It shows that you have home-training and some class.

Do you think that you eat like a caveman? Why do you think having proper eating etiquette is important?

_____

_____

_____

_____

_____

_____

_____

_____

_____

_____

_____

_____

_____

_____

_____

15.

Chew Gum With Discretion

When chewing gum, keep in mind your surroundings and chew accordingly. Loud gum chewing and popping is not gentleman-like and can be annoying.

Are you guilty of chewing gum loudly? Do you know people who are? Why should you be mindful of your surroundings in general?

_____

_____

_____

_____

_____

_____

_____

_____

_____

_____

_____

_____

_____

_____

16.

Thank You Will Suffice

If you are offered a gift, accept it and say thank you. The person took out the time to think about you and you should repay them with courtesy. In most cases you can never go wrong with saying thank you.

How many times do you say thank you in a day? Do you consider yourself to be grateful?

_____

_____

_____

_____

_____

_____

_____

_____

_____

_____

_____

_____

_____

_____

_____

_____

17.

Cell Phone Etiquette

When talking on the phone, everyone around you doesn't want to hear your conversation. You shouldn't be swearing, talking loud and acting belligerent. If you have to take a phone call, go to a quiet place so you can hear and not distract others.

How would you feel if you were talking to a group of people and someone in the middle of your conversation gets on their phone and starts having a conversation?

_____

_____

_____

_____

_____

_____

_____

_____

_____

_____

_____

_____

_____

_____

_____

18.

Basic Suit Colors

Purchase a black and grey suit to cover all occasions where a suit is necessary. You can never go wrong with these two colors. Make sure that you know your suit size so you can buy a suit that fits.

Do you have a grey or black suit? Do you know your suit size? How can you find out your suit size?

_____

_____

_____

_____

_____

_____

_____

_____

_____

_____

_____

_____

_____

_____

_____

_____

19.

A Tailored Suit, Can't GoWrong

Wear a suit and tie to a job

interview and make sure that it's

tailored to fit you. This is the

employer's first impression of you.

A sloppy suit is not a good suit.

Period.

Do you know what it feels like to wear a tailored suit? Do you know of any tailors in your area?

_____

_____

_____

_____

_____

_____

_____

_____

_____

_____

_____

_____

_____

_____

_____

_____

_____

20.

Keep Time
With A Watch

Wear a watch to keep the time. Your

cell phone is mainly used to

communicate not check the time.

Besides, wearing a watch is more

mature and says that you value

your time.

How many people do you know own a watch? Do you prefer to wear a watch or use your phone to keep track of time? Why?

_____

_____

_____

_____

_____

_____

_____

_____

_____

_____

_____

_____

_____

_____

_____

_____

_____

21.

Speak Life

Speak in a positive tone with positive words. If you don't have anything good to say then don't say anything at all. Sometimes it's just better to keep your thoughts to yourself.

Do you speak life or death in your daily conversations with people? How often do you offer an encouraging word?

_____

_____

_____

_____

_____

_____

_____

_____

_____

_____

_____

_____

_____

_____

_____

_____

22.

The Infamous Belt

Wear a belt. You know why. Nobody wants to see your underwear. It is downright disgusting and can give off mixed signals to observers. Make sure you wear a belt that fits and use it for what it was intended for. To keep your pants up.

Why wear a belt that doesn't hold your pants up? Why is sagging popular?

_____

_____

_____

_____

_____

_____

_____

_____

_____

_____

_____

_____

_____

_____

_____

_____

_____

_____

23.

The Handkerchief

Rock a handkerchief in your suit chest pocket that pops and makes a statement. It's the gentleman's accessory piece and can be a great item for conversation. Stand out from the crowd.

Do you know how to fold a handkerchief into a pocket square? What other accessories can you use as a compliment to your suit?

_____

_____

_____

_____

_____

_____

_____

_____

_____

_____

_____

_____

_____

_____

_____

_____

_____

_____

24.

Nothing Like a Nice Pair of Shoes

Buy a pair of brown and black lace up shoes. They go with everything and are an all-time classic. Every man should own a pair of black and brown lace up shoes.

Do you own a nice pair of black or brown lace up shoes? Do you know where to find a pair?

_____

_____

_____

_____

_____

_____

_____

_____

_____

_____

_____

_____

_____

_____

_____

_____

_____

25.

A Father's Wisdom

Have a relationship with your father/father-figure. They are where you want to be and it's wise to listen to them. It's important to have them in your life as a foundation.

Remember, one day you will be a father too.

Do you have a relationship with your father? Why or why not? Do you have a positive role model in your life?

_____

_____

_____

_____

_____

_____

_____

_____

_____

_____

_____

_____

_____

_____

_____

_____

_____

_____

26.

Forgiveness Sets You Free

Forgive those who hurt you. Don't listen to what popular culture says because real men forgive. Be the bigger man and take the first step to forgive those who have done wrong to you. Just think, at some point in your life you will have to ask for forgiveness.

Do you have someone in your life that you have not forgiven? Do you think forgiveness is important?

_____

_____

_____

_____

_____

_____

_____

_____

_____

_____

_____

_____

_____

_____

_____

27.

Honor Thy Father and Thy Mother

Take care of your parents whenever you can simply because they are your parents. They brought you into this world and for that you are indebted to them. Honor them every chance you can while they are alive. Give them their flowers while they can enjoy them.

What are some ways you can honor your parents?

_____

_____

_____

_____

_____

_____

_____

_____

_____

_____

_____

_____

_____

_____

_____

_____

_____

_____

28.

Leaders Read, A lot

Read everyday for at least 20 minutes a day. Pick up a book, read the newspaper or an article online. Read something that is stimulating and makes you think. Reading feeds your mind and allows for great conversation. Men are readers and so are leaders.

What's your favorite book to read? Do you have a favorite subject or genre?

_____

_____

_____

_____

_____

_____

_____

_____

_____

_____

_____

_____

_____

_____

_____

_____

29.

Hats Are For Outside

When you walk into a building you should take off your hat because it is a sign of respect. Hats were designed to cover your head from the elements by keeping your head warm in the winter or providing shade in the summer.

What is your take on wearing hats inside a building? Do you think this unwritten rule is old-fashioned?

_____
_____
_____
_____
_____
_____
_____
_____
_____
_____
_____
_____
_____
_____
_____
_____

30.
Don't Just Talk About It, Be About It

Gentlemen practice what they preach by always assessing their own behaviors and accepting constructive criticisms. Always be sure to follow up your words with action so people will take you seriously. Real men take responsibility for their words and actions.

What does it mean to "follow through"? Can you recall a time you followed through with what you said you were going to do? What was the outcome?

_____

_____

_____

_____

_____

_____

_____

_____

_____

_____

_____

_____

_____

_____

_____

_____

_____

_____

Call To Action

Now that you have finished this book, take some time to reflect on what you have read. Really internalize it and then begin to take action. No one ever remembers everything they have read unless they have an extreme case of photographic memory. Keep this book with you and read it again to jog your memory. I hope that you have enjoyed reading this book as much as I have enjoyed writing it. Please feel free to take notes on the things that you have read. I've provided you with space to write down your thoughts and answer the questions. Best wishes on your journey to being a 21st century gentleman.

Gentleman's Notes

Gentleman's Notes

Gentleman's Notes

Gentleman's Notes

Gentleman's Notes

Made in the USA
Lexington, KY
18 November 2014